# THE STORY
# BABE
# RUTH

## A Biography Book for New Readers

—— Written by ——
**Jenna Grodzicki**

—Illustrated by—
**Ellen Surrey**

**R**

ROCKRIDGE
PRESS

For Tanner, my favorite baseball player

Series Designer: Angela Navarra
Interior and Cover Designer: Lisa Forde
Art Producer: Hannah Dickerson
Editor: Mary Colgan
Production Editor: Rachel Taenzler
Production Manager: Michael Kay

Illustrations © 2021 Ellen Surrey. Photography © Library of Congress Prints and Photographs Division, Bain News Service photograph collection/LC-DIG-ggbain-33131, p. 50; Archive World/Alamy Stock Photo, p. 51; PictureLux/The Hollywood Archive/Alamy Stock Photo, p. 52. All maps used under license from Creative Market. Author photo courtesy of Greta Lindquist-Merlino. Illustrator photo courtesy of Jessica Watkins.

ISBN: Print 978-1-64876-599-5 | eBook 978-1-63807-602-5
R0

# ⇒ CONTENTS ⇐

CHAPTER 1

A LEGEND IS BORN

# ⚾ Meet Babe Ruth ⚾

*CRACK!* It's going, going, gone!

It was the 1926 **World Series**. Babe Ruth and the New York Yankees were up against the St. Louis Cardinals. Babe had promised a sick little boy named Johnny Sylvester that he would hit a home run just for him. And he did. Three home runs in one game!

That's just who Babe was. He had a big heart. He cared about his fans, especially the children. A few days later, Babe surprised Johnny by showing up at his house. It was a dream come true for the young baseball fan. Johnny went on to make a full recovery.

But before Babe was a baseball hero, he was a poor boy from Baltimore, Maryland. He ran through the dirty streets, causing trouble, until he was sent to school at the age of seven.

It was there that Babe discovered he had a talent for baseball.

When Babe grew up, he played in the **major leagues**. He played for the Boston Red Sox and then the New York Yankees. No one had ever seen anyone hit the ball like Babe. He swung with all his might. He hit home run after home run. Fans screamed his name and cheered him on.

Being a **professional** ball player didn't stop Babe from making bad choices. But he always learned from his mistakes.

WHERE?

MARYLAND

★ BALTIMORE

VIRGINIA

Even though it's been almost 100 years since Babe played baseball, he hasn't been forgotten. He changed the way the game is played. Let's find out how a young boy from Baltimore went on to become one of the greatest players of all time.

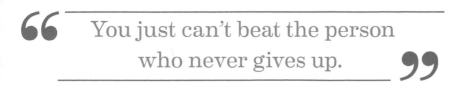

“ You just can't beat the person who never gives up. ”

# Babe's America

Babe was born on February 6, 1895, in Baltimore, Maryland. Big changes were happening in the United States at that time. The economy was still feeling the effects of the **Industrial Revolution**, and many people were moving from farms to the cities. Things that used to be made by hand were now made in large amounts by machines in big factories. Light bulbs,

telephones, and automobiles had recently been invented.

These new inventions cost a lot of money, though. Most families couldn't afford them, and most homes did not have electricity. Television had not been invented yet. Instead, people read newspapers to find out what was happening in the world around them.

**JUMP -IN THE- THINK TANK**

Baseball was Babe's favorite sport. What is your favorite sport? Why do you like it?

Baltimore was a major **seaport**. Ships came and went, carrying goods to people all over the world. The city was also a railroad hub. Its many railways connected Baltimore to other parts of the country. The city was bustling. In their spare time, people turned to sports for entertainment.

Baseball was becoming very popular, and many professional teams started playing in cities all over the country. People read the newspapers to follow their favorite team. The teams that won usually had great pitchers. It was rare for a batter to hit a home run. Local kids and adults played baseball in fields or in the streets. Going to the ballpark was a fun thing for families to do, too. Baseball became America's national **pastime**. In 1903, professional teams played in the first World Series. Baseball fans of all ages rushed to watch the games. People without tickets sometimes even climbed walls to see the players in action.

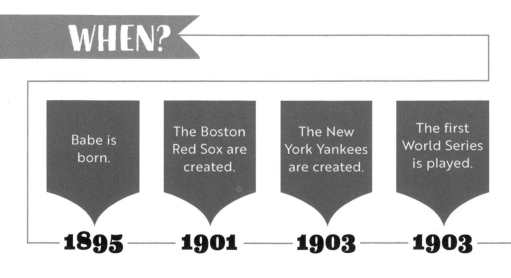

## WHEN?

| Babe is born. | The Boston Red Sox are created. | The New York Yankees are created. | The first World Series is played. |
| --- | --- | --- | --- |
| **1895** | **1901** | **1903** | **1903** |

# CHAPTER 2

# THE EARLY YEARS

# The Streets of Baltimore

Babe Ruth was the oldest of eight children. Six of his brothers and sisters died very young, and only his younger sister, Mamie, lived to be an adult. When he was born, his parents named him George Herman Ruth, Jr. He was given the nickname "Babe" later in life.

Babe's mother was named Kate. His father was also named George, and people called him "Big George." The family lived in a small apartment above a bar that Big George owned and ran. The neighborhood where the Ruth family lived was called Pigtown. This was a fitting name because pigs often ran through the streets. The pigs were brought in on trains and were herded to the nearby butcher house.

Big George worked long hours at the bar, and Kate was sick a lot. They didn't have much time to look after their son. So, Babe was free to do whatever he wanted. He spent a lot of time in the streets. He was always on the lookout for something fun to do.

Sometimes Babe made good choices, like playing games with friends, including baseball. Other times, Babe's choices weren't so good. He got into fights. He stole fruit from street shops. He threw tomatoes at passing wagons. He took money from the cash register at his father's bar. And he refused to go to school. Babe's parents didn't know how to get him to behave. When he was seven years old, they decided to send Babe away to a boarding school.

# The School for Wayward Boys

On June 13, 1902, Babe arrived at St. Mary's Industrial School for Boys. St. Mary's was a school for orphans and wayward boys, or troublemakers. Parents could bring their sons to St. Mary's if they caused too much

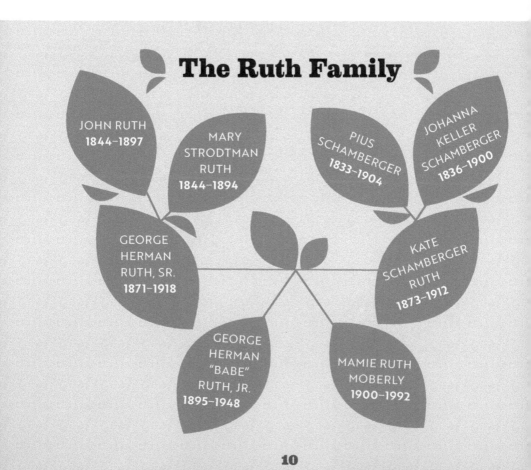

## The Ruth Family

JOHN RUTH
1844–1897

MARY STRODTMAN RUTH
1844–1894

PIUS SCHAMBERGER
1833–1904

JOHANNA KELLER SCHAMBERGER
1836–1900

GEORGE HERMAN RUTH, SR.
1871–1918

KATE SCHAMBERGER RUTH
1873–1912

GEORGE HERMAN "BABE" RUTH, JR.
1895–1948

MAMIE RUTH MOBERLY
1900–1992

trouble at home. At first, Babe did not like being at St. Mary's. He missed his family, and he couldn't spend all day doing whatever he wanted. St. Mary's had a lot of rules. The boys slept in big rooms. Their beds were arranged in neat rows. The teachers woke them up early every morning. The younger boys focused on reading and writing. The older boys learned how to be bakers, farmers, carpenters, or **tailors**.

But St. Mary's had something Babe loved—baseball. One of the teachers, Brother Matthias, arranged the boys into teams. In the afternoons, they played ball. Babe worked hard, and soon he was a star batter and, later, pitcher.

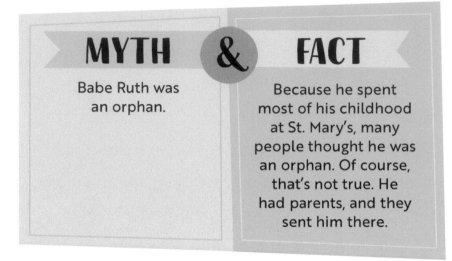

**MYTH & FACT**

Babe Ruth was an orphan.

Because he spent most of his childhood at St. Mary's, many people thought he was an orphan. Of course, that's not true. He had parents, and they sent him there.

Brother Matthias would become one of the most important people in Babe's life. He saw great things in Babe. He knew the boy just needed someone to care for him. He became a **mentor** to Babe. He helped him with baseball and his schoolwork. Babe looked up to him.

Babe spent most of the next 10 years at St. Mary's. He moved home with his family a few times, but it never lasted long. Sadly, Babe's mother died when Babe was only 17. He didn't move home again after that.

By the time Babe was 19, he was training to become a tailor. In the afternoons, he was St. Mary's star pitcher. But his life was about to change. At the time, Maryland had a **minor league** baseball team called the Baltimore Orioles. When the team's owner, Jack Dunn, saw him play, he signed Babe right away. Babe would play for the Orioles.

JUMP
—IN THE—
THINK TANK

How can someone believing in you change your life?

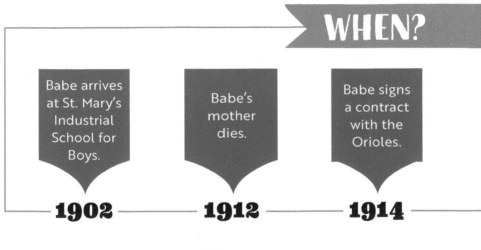

WHEN?

Babe arrives at St. Mary's Industrial School for Boys.

Babe's mother dies.

Babe signs a contract with the Orioles.

**1902** — **1912** — **1914**

# CHAPTER 3

# PLAYING

# PROFESSIONAL BALL

# ⚾ In the Minor Leagues ⚾

At just 19 years old, Babe signed his first
professional baseball **contract**. He was going to
be paid $600 a season to pitch for the Orioles.
Today, that would be like getting paid $15,000.
Babe couldn't believe it! He was going to be *paid*
to play baseball? It was a dream come true.

On February 27, 1914, Babe said goodbye to his
friends at St. Mary's. He soon boarded a train
with the rest of his new team. They were headed
to Fayetteville, North Carolina, where the players
would practice together. Babe Ruth was on his
way to his first spring training.

For Babe, everything was new and exciting.
He had never been on a train before. He had
never even left Baltimore. When they arrived
in Fayetteville, Babe marveled at the warm
weather. At the hotel, he was in for another
surprise. The team ate their meals in the hotel

restaurant, and the Orioles paid the bill. Babe
could order whatever he wanted! This was huge
for a boy who had been fed stew and bread every
day at St. Mary's. That first morning, Babe ate
three stacks of pancakes and three helpings of
ham. His teammates couldn't believe how much
he ate. The hotel had something else Babe had
never seen before—an elevator. He rode it up and
down, up and down.

Babe couldn't get enough of the trains.
Every morning, he got up extra early to watch
the trains go through the station. But he was

always back at the hotel in time to be first in line for breakfast. Babe's world had never been more exciting.

##  "Babe" Is Born

Babe's teammates saw how excited he got over every new thing. And they knew he was only 19 years old. When Babe walked onto the field for the first time, wearing his new uniform and a big grin on his face, the older players laughed. One story has it that the players called him Jack Dunn's "new babe." The name stuck, and soon everyone was calling him "Babe."

During spring training, Babe hit the first home run of his professional career. The ball flew over the fence and landed in a cornfield. The players and coaches were impressed. After all, Babe was a **rookie** and a pitcher, too. Pitchers weren't usually very good hitters.

> **"** Never let the fear of striking out
> keep you from playing the game. **"**

The team returned to Baltimore for the start of the season. On April 22, 1914, Babe pitched in his first regular season game, against a team called the Buffalo Bisons. He led the Orioles to a 6–0 win.

With his first paycheck, Babe bought a motorcycle. He flew down the streets. He visited his friends at St. Mary's. Jack worried Babe would crash. He urged him to get rid of the

WHERE? VIRGINIA
NORTH CAROLINA
FAYETTEVILLE

motorcycle. But nothing could keep Babe off that bike.

As the season went on, Babe continued to pitch well. More often than not, his pitching led the Orioles to victory. When he was at bat, he didn't always get a hit. But when he did, watch out! He hit the ball farther than anybody else. In June, Babe and the Orioles went on a winning streak. Thirteen wins in a row!

JUMP
–IN THE–
THINK
TANK

Getting paid to play baseball was a dream come true for Babe. What is your dream job?

19

But the Orioles hardly had any fans. Baltimore also had a major league team, the Terrapins. The people of Baltimore chose to go to that team's games instead. It didn't help that the Terrapins' stadium was right across the street from where the Orioles played. With few ticket sales, Jack was losing money fast. So, he traded some of his best players, including Babe. Soon, Babe was headed to Boston to play for the Red Sox.

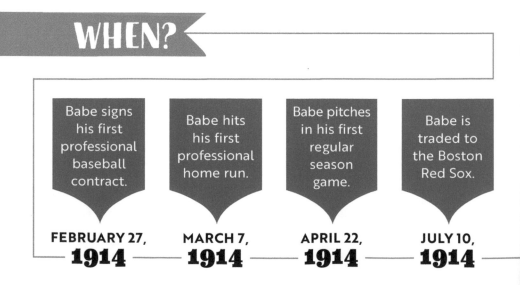

## WHEN?

| Babe signs his first professional baseball contract. | Babe hits his first professional home run. | Babe pitches in his first regular season game. | Babe is traded to the Boston Red Sox. |
|---|---|---|---|
| **FEBRUARY 27, 1914** | **MARCH 7, 1914** | **APRIL 22, 1914** | **JULY 10, 1914** |

Ruth

CHAPTER 4

MAKING HISTORY

# The Boston Red Sox

On the morning of July 11, 1914, Babe arrived in Boston, eager to start his major league career. Later that day, he played in his first game with the Red Sox. They were up against the Cleveland Naps (now called the Cleveland Guardians). Babe pitched a good game, and the Red Sox won 4–3. But Babe didn't pitch so well in his next game. And for the next month, Babe sat on the bench. He didn't play in a single game.

Babe's teammates didn't know what to think of him. He was loud and confident. He liked to play jokes. And he called everyone "Kid." Their biggest problem with Babe, however, was that he wanted to do **batting practice**. Babe was a pitcher, so his teammates didn't think he belonged at batting practice. But he kept showing up. One day, Babe came to the park to find all his bats had been sawed in half.

In August, the owner of the Red Sox sent Babe to Rhode Island to play for his minor league team, the Providence Grays. He thought Babe could help the Grays win their league's **pennant**, or championship. Babe was not happy. He worried his major league career was over before it really began. And he also missed his girlfriend, Helen. But Providence wasn't all bad. After sitting on the bench in Boston for a month, Babe got to play again. And Babe did indeed help the Grays win that pennant.

Babe returned to Boston in October, and he and Helen were soon married. Then 19-year-old Babe and his 17-year-old bride moved to a small apartment in Baltimore for the off-season.

# Pitcher at Bat

Babe was back with the Red Sox in the spring of 1915. On May 6, they played the Yankees in New York. Babe stepped up to the plate. When the ball came his way, he swung hard and *CRACK!* The ball soared through the air and landed in the upper right field stands. It was Babe's first major league home run! Back then, home runs were rare. And for a pitcher to hit one? That was unheard of. Fans started paying attention and cheering just for him.

Babe had proved to the world that he was one of the best pitchers in baseball. But by 1918, he didn't want to pitch anymore. Babe's coach knew he was a talented hitter, but he needed Babe on the mound, too. So, Babe continued to do both.

Late in the 1918 season, Babe got some sad news. His father had died. Neither of his parents would ever see the baseball hero he would become.

When the 1919 season came around, Babe got his wish. He pitched less and less, and had more opportunities to hit. On May 20, his mighty swing made history. He hit the first **grand slam** of his career.

WHERE?

BOSTON

PROVIDENCE

RHODE ISLAND

MASSACHUSETTS

BALTIMORE

MARYLAND

**MYTH & FACT**

The Baby Ruth candy bar is named after Babe Ruth.

The Baby Ruth candy bar is officially named after Ruth Cleveland, the daughter of former US president Grover Cleveland.

A grand slam is when the batter hits a home run when the bases are loaded with runners. This means there's a player on every base. This scores four runs all at the same time.

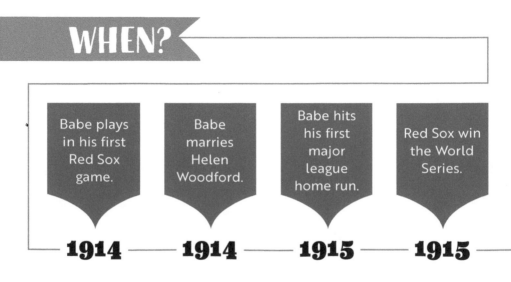

**WHEN?**

Babe plays in his first Red Sox game.

Babe marries Helen Woodford.

Babe hits his first major league home run.

Red Sox win the World Series.

1914 — 1914 — 1915 — 1915

By this time, Babe had helped the Red Sox win three World Series championships. He had become a **celebrity**. Baseball fans everywhere knew his name. He spent money on expensive things, like cars and fancy clothes. He was also very generous. He donated money to orphanages and hospitals. He even bought a car for his old mentor, Brother Matthias.

It seemed like Babe would have a long and successful career with the Red Sox. But that was about to change. In 1920, Babe was traded to the New York Yankees.

JUMP
—IN THE—
THINK
TANK

What is something you've done that you are very proud of? Why?

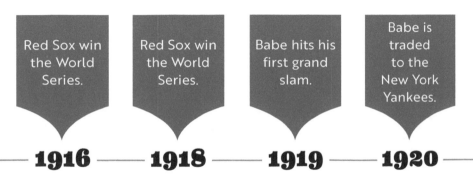

| 1916 | 1918 | 1919 | 1920 |
|------|------|------|------|
| Red Sox win the World Series. | Red Sox win the World Series. | Babe hits his first grand slam. | Babe is traded to the New York Yankees. |

# CHAPTER 5

# BABE IN THE BIG APPLE

# Changing the Game

When Babe joined the New York Yankees, they hoped his all-star hitting would help them become a winning team. Babe had been happy in Boston, but he promised to play just as hard for the Yankees.

Babe started the season with strikeout after strikeout. But by May, he was back to hitting home runs. Fans loved watching him smash the ball out of the park. Babe swung the bat so hard that when he missed, he spun all the way around. The fans liked watching that, too. Babe's picture was in all the newspapers. Reporters gave him lots of nicknames, like the Colossus of Swat and the King of Crash. Other players tried to copy Babe's swing. They wanted to hit home runs, too. Games started to be won by runs scored, not just from pitchers striking out batters. Baseball was changing.

Babe loved living in New York City. When
he wasn't playing baseball, he found lots of fun
things to do. He went to parties and stayed out
all night. He bought cars and drove them too
fast. He ate and ate and ate some more. But
Helen was unhappy. She didn't enjoy being in
the spotlight like her husband. So, she moved
to the farmhouse in Massachusetts where she
and Babe lived in the off-season.

As the season went on, Babe continued to hit home runs. Soon, he passed his record of 29 from the previous season: 51 . . . 52 . . . 53 . . . 54! Babe ended his first season with the Yankees with a record-breaking 54 home runs!

## JUMP —IN THE— THINK TANK

Babe loved helping children in need. Why do you think that is?

## Babe at Bat

What's better than 54 home runs in one season? 59! In 1921, Babe broke his own record by hitting 59 home runs. And he helped the Yankees make it to their first ever World Series appearance. Even though they didn't win, just getting there was a huge **accomplishment**.

That year was a big year for Babe off the field as well. His daughter, Dorothy, was born. The next year was a different story. In 1922, Babe was out of shape from eating too much, and he had a terrible season. He argued with the **umpires** and his teammates. He got thrown out of a few games. When the season was over, the future mayor of New York told Babe he had let everyone down, especially the children who looked up to him.

Babe knew he had to do better. He spent the off-season with Helen and Dorothy on their farm in Sudbury, Massachusetts. He got in shape by chopping wood, ice skating, and taking care of the animals. He and Helen went for long walks in the woods with Dorothy riding on his shoulders.

When Babe returned to New York for the 1923 season, he was ready to play ball. On April 18,

the team played their first game at their new home, Yankee Stadium. More than 60,000 fans filled the stands. When Babe was at bat, he swung with everything he had. *CRACK!* The ball flew across the field and landed in the stands. Babe had hit Yankee Stadium's first home run. Later, a reporter nicknamed the ballpark "The House That Ruth Built." The nickname stuck.

WHERE?

SUDBURY

MASSACHUSETTS
NEW YORK

NEW YORK CITY

> I swing big, with everything I've got. I hit big or I miss big. I like to live as big as I can.

Babe was unstoppable that season. The Yankees went on to win the 1923 championship. This was the first World Series win for the team. Babe was named MVP (most valuable player). He was a bigger star than ever!

## WHEN?

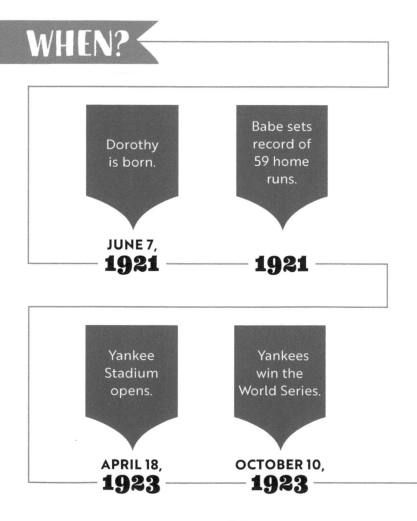

Dorothy is born.

**JUNE 7, 1921**

Babe sets record of 59 home runs.

**1921**

Yankee Stadium opens.

**APRIL 18, 1923**

Yankees win the World Series.

**OCTOBER 10, 1923**

# CHAPTER 6

## UNSTOPPABLE

# ⚾ Ups and Downs ⚾

For the next few years, Babe's life was like a roller coaster. In 1924, he played well and hit a total of 46 home runs. But Babe soon went back to his old ways. He ate too many unhealthy foods. He stayed out all night every night. Babe treated life like one big party.

In April 1925, Babe collapsed and was taken to the hospital. He had a serious problem with his stomach. The doctor said it was because he wasn't taking care of himself. Babe spent six weeks in the hospital recovering. When he got out, it

WHERE?

NEW YORK

NEW JERSEY

NEW YORK CITY

was baseball all day and parties all night. His performance on the field suffered. The coaches tried to get him to behave. But Babe just wanted to have fun.

Around this time, Helen decided that she didn't want to be married to Babe anymore. Their marriage was over, and it seemed that Babe's days as a home run hero were over, too.

Babe knew he had to change if he wanted to get back on top. He apologized to his team and his fans. That winter, he worked out at a gym to get back in shape. When spring training came around, he was healthier than he had been in years.

Babe's hard work paid off. He helped the Yankees make it to the 1926 World Series. Although they didn't win, Babe hit three home runs in one of the games! The Sultan of Swat was back and better than ever.

The following year, Babe made history. He broke his home run record with a whopping 60 in one season!

## ⚾ The Last at Bat ⚾

Babe and Helen had been living apart for several years when he got some sad news. Helen passed away in January 1929. Soon after, Babe married

## MYTH & FACT

A baseball signed by Babe Ruth is worth a lot of money.

Although it is valuable, Babe signed so many baseballs over his career that it's not worth as much as people might think.

a woman named Claire Hodgson. The new family now included Babe, Claire, Julia (Claire's daughter), and Dorothy. They all moved into a fancy apartment in New York City.

JUMP
—IN THE—
THINK
TANK

What does it mean that Babe's life was like a roller coaster?

Babe continued to deliver big hits. His most famous home run of all came during game three of the 1932 World Series. The Yankees were playing the Chicago Cubs. When Babe came up to bat, the Cubs' players and their fans shouted insults. After two strikes, Babe raised his arm and pointed toward center field. When the next pitch came, Babe smashed the ball right to that exact spot! He ran around the bases, laughing all the way. Did Babe actually point to where he was planning to hit the ball? Or was he just teasing the fans and the home run was a coincidence? Nobody knows for sure, and people still argue about it. To this day, baseball fans refer to his

famous home run as the "Called Shot." The Yankees went on to win that World Series in four straight games.

In 1934, Babe was almost 40 years old. That's a long career for a baseball player. He was slowing down. Before the 1935 season

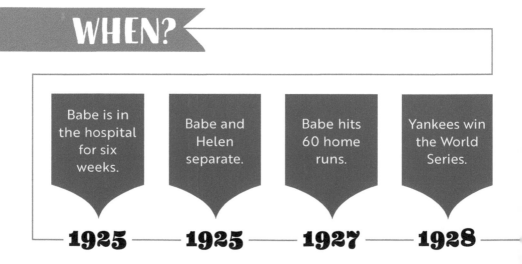

**WHEN?**

| Babe is in the hospital for six weeks. | Babe and Helen separate. | Babe hits 60 home runs. | Yankees win the World Series. |
| --- | --- | --- | --- |
| **1925** | **1925** | **1927** | **1928** |

began, the Yankees traded him to the Boston
Braves. On opening day, Babe hit a home run.
But after that, things started to go downhill. His
best baseball playing days were behind him, and
he knew it.

On May 25, Babe hit his final three home
runs in a game against the Pittsburgh Pirates.
That brought his career total to an incredible
714 home runs. He played in his last game on
May 30 and officially retired a few days later.
He never played professional baseball again.

Babe marries Claire Hodgson.

Babe hits his famous "Called Shot."

Yankees win the World Series.

Babe plays in his last professional game.

**1929** ── **1932** ── **1932** ── **1935**

CHAPTER 7

# THE LEGEND LIVES ON

# ⚾ Hall of Famer ⚾

For 22 seasons, baseball had been Babe's whole world. When he retired, he needed to find something else to do; so, he took up golf. Babe played golf all the time. When it was too cold to golf, Babe went hunting or bowling. Still, Babe missed baseball. He wanted to become a team manager. But no one would hire him. Team owners didn't trust him to be a good leader because of his past behavior.

In 1936, the National Baseball Hall of Fame was established in Cooperstown, New York.

Babe was among the first five players to be **inducted**. This was a huge honor.

In 1938, Babe was asked to coach first base for the Brooklyn Dodgers. He jumped at the chance to be part of the sport again. Unfortunately, it lasted only one season. Babe didn't get along with the Dodgers' new manager, so he didn't return the following year.

66 Baseball was, is, and always will be to me the best game in the world. 99

Babe continued to play golf and spend time with his family. On April 27, 1947, the Yankees hosted "Babe Ruth Day." More than 58,000 fans cheered for the home run king. One of those fans was Johnny Sylvester, the boy Babe had hit those home runs for back in 1926. Johnny was all grown up and the president of a big company. He thanked Babe for visiting him when he was sick all those years ago. But now Babe was the one who was sick. He had throat cancer.

A year later, Babe made his final appearance at the ballpark. It was Yankee Stadium's 25th anniversary, and Babe's jersey number 3 was being retired. That meant no other Yankee player would ever wear the number 3. Babe looked frail as he walked onto the field, using a bat as a cane.

Two months later, on August 16, 1948, Babe passed away. He was only 53 years old.

**JUMP
—IN THE—
THINK
TANK**

What do you think was Babe's greatest accomplishment? Why do you think that?

#  World Class ⚾

Babe Ruth was a legend. When he retired, he held 54 major league records. In his 22 seasons of professional baseball, he won seven World Series championships. And he hit 714 home runs, a record that stood for almost 40 years. In 1974, Hank Aaron of the Atlanta Braves became the first to break it, eventually hitting 755 home runs. Today, Babe is in third place for most home runs of all time. Only Hank and Barry Bonds (762) have hit more.

But Babe was so much more than a baseball player. He helped pick the world up during the years of the **Great Depression**. He brought joy and entertainment to people's lives. And he brought hope to children everywhere. Whether he was helping the boys at St. Mary's, visiting sick children in hospitals, or signing autographs for every child who asked, Babe was a real-life hero. He showed everyone that it was possible to come from nothing and make it all the way to the top.

Before he died, he started the Babe Ruth Foundation. Money donated to this foundation went to help poor and needy children. When he passed away, most of Babe's money went to the foundation, too.

Babe wasn't perfect. His life had its share of ups and downs. But no matter how bad things got, he always picked himself back up. He learned from his mistakes, and he never gave up.

Ask any baseball fan who the greatest player of all time is, and chances are they'll say, "Babe Ruth." He changed the game forever.

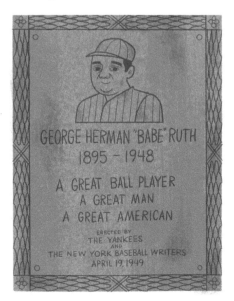

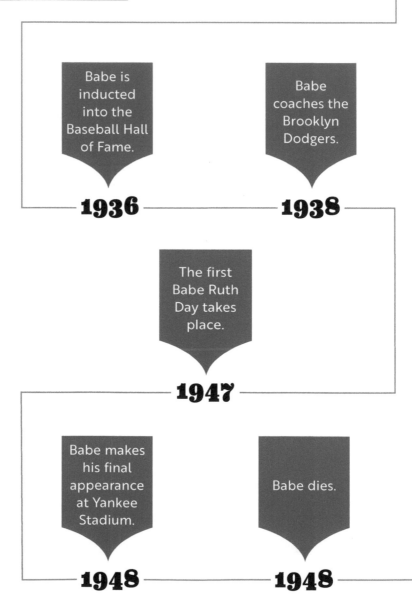

Babe is inducted into the Baseball Hall of Fame.

Babe coaches the Brooklyn Dodgers.

**1936** — **1938**

The first Babe Ruth Day takes place.

**1947**

Babe makes his final appearance at Yankee Stadium.

Babe dies.

**1948** — **1948**

# CHAPTER 8

# SO . . . WHO WAS BABE RUTH ?

# Challenge Accepted

Now that you've learned all about Babe Ruth, let's take a little quiz! Here are 10 questions to test your new knowledge. Feel free to look back in the book to find the answers if you need to, but try to remember first!

**1** **Where was Babe born?**
→ A Boston
→ B New York City
→ C Baltimore
→ D Providence

**2** **What was Babe's real name?**
→ A Jack
→ B Hank
→ C Barry
→ D George

**3** Who was the first person
Babe felt believed in him?

→ A    Brother Matthias

→ B    George Ruth, Sr.

→ C    Kate Ruth

→ D    Helen Woodford

**4** Which team did Babe first play for?

→ A    Boston Braves

→ B    Boston Red Sox

→ C    Baltimore Orioles

→ D    New York Yankees

**5** When was Babe traded to the Yankees?

→ A    1895

→ B    1914

→ C    1920

→ D    1926

**6** Why was Babe known as an American legend?

A He could eat more than anyone else.

B He hit more home runs than anyone else.

C He drove faster than anyone else.

D He played golf better than anyone else.

**7** How many home runs did Babe hit in his career?

A 704

B 714

C 724

D 734

**8** When did Babe retire from baseball?

A 1935

B 1930

C 1925

D 1920

**9** **What were some of Babe's biggest accomplishments?**

→ A He was a talented pitcher.

→ B He set many home run records.

→ C He helped children in need.

→ D All of the above.

**10** **Who was the first person to break Babe's all-time home run record?**

→ A Hank Aaron

→ B David Ortiz

→ C Barry Bonds

→ D Jackie Robinson

# Our World

It's been more than 80 years since Babe last played baseball. But his greatness has not been forgotten. Let's take a look at some of the ways Babe's work is still having an impact today.

→ After Babe left, the Red Sox didn't win another World Series for 86 years! Everyone said the team was cursed because Babe had been traded to the Yankees. They called it the "Curse of the Bambino." *Bambino* means "baby" in Italian. Many people still believe that trading Babe Ruth was the worst decision in baseball history.

→ Babe paved the way for the home run stars of today. When other players copied his mighty swing, they started to hit home runs, too. Today, if a player hits a really big home run, it is described as "Ruthian."

→ The Babe Ruth League was created 70 years ago for children who want to play baseball or softball. It was named after Babe and combines two of his favorite things: baseball and supporting children. Today, kids all over the country play the sport he loved under his name.

## JUMP —IN THE— THINK TANK FOR MORE!

Now let's think a little bit more about Babe's life and how he changed the world.

→ Babe's life changed when he was sent to St. Mary's Industrial School for Boys. How do you think his life would have turned out if he hadn't gone there? Do you think he would have gone on to become one of the greatest baseball players of all time?

→ Babe made some mistakes in his life. But he always found a way to make things right. Think about a time you made a mistake. What did you do to make things better?

→ Babe was a hero to many people. Who is your hero? Why do you look up to that person?

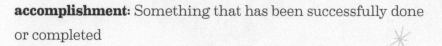

# Glossary

**accomplishment:** Something that has been successfully done or completed

**batting practice:** The time before a game starts when players can work on their swings and practice hitting

**celebrity:** A person who is famous

**contract:** A piece of paper that shows an agreement between two or more people and is supported by the law

**grand slam:** A home run when all the bases are loaded with runners, meaning there's one player on each base; it scores four runs

**Great Depression:** The period of time during the 1930s when much of the world faced harsh economic conditions; many people were out of work, hungry, or homeless

**inducted:** Officially included someone as a member

**Industrial Revolution:** A time in the United States when things that used to be made by hand were now made in large amounts by machines in big factories

**major leagues:** The highest level of professional baseball in the United States

**mentor:** Someone who plays an important role in another person's life as a guide and teacher

**minor league:** A league of professional baseball teams that plays below the highest level

**pastime:** An activity or hobby that people enjoy

**pennant:** A flag that is given to the best baseball team in the league

**professional:** Getting paid for doing a job

**rookie:** An athlete in their first season on a team

**seaport:** A city or town where ships that travel on the sea can dock, load, and unload

**tailors:** People who make, change, or fix clothing

**umpires:** The officials at baseball games who make sure the players and coaches follow the rules

**World Series:** The baseball championship, when the two best teams play games until one of the two teams wins four games total; this happens at the end of every baseball season and is meant to decide which team is the best in all of baseball

# Bibliography

BabeRuth.com: www.baberuth.com Accessed April 21, 2021.

Babe Ruth Central: www.baberuthcentral.com Accessed April 21, 2021.

Christopher, Matt. *Babe Ruth: Legends in Sports*. New York: Little, Brown and Company, 2005.

Considine, Bob and Babe Ruth. *The Babe Ruth Story*. New York: E.P. Dutton & Co., Inc., 1948.

Creamer, Robert W. *Babe: The Legend Comes to Life*. New York: Simon & Schuster Paperbacks, 1974.

Gilbert, Brother, C.F.X. *Young Babe Ruth: His Early Life and Baseball Career, from the Memoirs of a Xaverian Brother*. Edited by Harry Rothgerber. North Carolina: McFarland & Company, Inc., 1999.

Hampton, Wilborn. *Up Close: Babe Ruth*. New York: Viking, 2009.

Hirshon, Nicholas. "Babe Ruth's Home Run Vow to Sick Jersey Boy Confirmed." *New York Daily News*. June 19, 2008. https://www.nydailynews .com/sports/baseball/yankees/babe-ruth-home-run-vow-sick-jersey-boy -confirmed-article-1.293847

Holub, Joan. *Who Was Babe Ruth?* New York: Penguin Workshop, 2012.

Leavy, Jane. *The Big Fella: Babe Ruth and the World He Created*. New York: HarperCollins Publishers, 2018.

Montville, Leigh. *The Big Bam: The Life and Times of Babe Ruth*. New York: Doubleday, 2006.

National Baseball Hall of Fame: www.baseballhall.org Accessed April 21, 2021.

Pirone, Dorothy Ruth (with Chris Martens). *My Dad, The Babe: Growing Up With an American Hero*. Boston: Quinlan Press, 1988.

Ruth, George Herman. *Babe Ruth's Own Book of Baseball*. New York: G.P. Putnam's Sons, 1928.

# Acknowledgments

I come from a long line of baseball fans. My nana and papa were huge Red Sox fans. My mother also cheers for the Red Sox, and my father's favorite team is the Phillies. I love the Red Sox, too (sorry, Dad), and I'm lucky to share that love with my family. When the opportunity to write about the legendary Babe Ruth came about, I had to take it. I'd like to thank my editor, Mary Colgan, for believing in my writing and helping make it shine. Big thanks to my husband, Shawn, and my children, Tessa and Tanner, for their love and support. I hope young readers will be inspired by Babe's story to dream big and always swing for the fences.

# About the Author

**Jenna Grodzicki** is the author of many fiction and nonfiction children's books. Her books include *I See Sea Food: Sea Creatures That Look Like Food* and *Harmony Humbolt: The Perfect Pets Queen*. Jenna lives near the beach with her husband, two kids, two cats, and one dog. She spent more than 10 years as an educator, but now she's a full-time writer. Jenna loves to read and go skiing with her family. To learn more, visit her website at JennaGrodzicki.com.

## About the Illustrator

**Ellen Surrey** makes her colorful illustrations out of sunny Los Angeles. Blending her love of mid-century design and vintage children's books, Ellen enjoys finding beauty in the past and sharing it with a contemporary audience. Her work has appeared in such publications as *The New York Times, The New Yorker*, and *The Los Angeles Times*. You can view more of her work by visiting EllenSurrey.com

# WHO WILL INSPIRE YOU NEXT?

EXPLORE A WORLD OF HEROES AND ROLE MODELS IN
***THE STORY OF...*** BIOGRAPHY SERIES FOR NEW READERS.

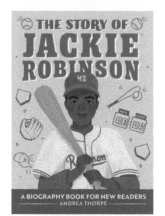

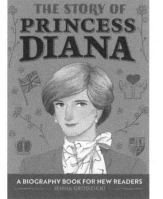

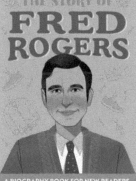

## → LOOK FOR THIS SERIES ←
### WHEREVER BOOKS AND EBOOKS ARE SOLD

Alexander Hamilton

Albert Einstein

Martin Luther King Jr.

George Washington

Jane Goodall

Barack Obama

Helen Keller

Marie Curie

Printed in the USA
CPSIA information can be obtained
at www.ICGtesting.com
CBHW081246200224
4500CB00007B/47

9 781648 765995